The Josefina Catherine Cunningham Memorial

HISTROIC UNSUNG FIGURES

Contents

Dedication

This book is dedicated to my three-year-old little sister Josefina Catherine Cunningham an African American girl who was murdered July 7th, 2023, by a white man named Robert J. Fisher in Rensselaer, New York. I want to preserve and honor her legacy as National African American History.

Have You Finished Your Course?

Introduction

I'm Jy'Quan Arnay Stewart. I was raised in Rensselaer, New York. I'm writing a story about my little sister Josefina Catherine Cunningham aka "Josie" an African American little girl who was murder on July 7th 2023 by Robert J. Fisher a white man in Rensselaer, New York while at our mother's house I was at my new apartment in Troy, New York when it happened. I remember seeing my little sister the night before Josefina's was perfectly fine and the next day, she was found dead with blue hands and lips. Blood was found on Josefina's bed. It had a powerful effect on me.

My sister was smiling and running around the day before she died. This powerful biography tells the story of my sister from the day she was born until the day of her death. My sister was three years old at the time of her death. She was a young and innocent African American little girl. God used my sister to show me that life is short, and we can die either young or old. The Bibles says in Hebrews Chapter 9 verse 27 KJV states:

"And as it is appointed unto men once to die, but after this the judgment."

I remember watching this man of God on YouTube. His name is Pastor Charles Lawson from Knoxville, Tennessee. He is an old-fashioned preacher. He was preaching on hell. He does not believe that babies go to hell because they are not accountable at that age. But he was saying no matter if your young, old, white, or black death is no respecter of persons. You can die at any time. Life is short.

I remember in the book of Second Timothy when Paul was in prison. Paul was coming to the end of his life, and he was facing death. Paul said, "I finished my course". What happens at the end of your life has a profound effect upon everyone. Like my sister Josefina, her death had a profound effect on the people in New York State. I believe this would be a powerful story to tell. Just like the story of Emmett Till. I believe her story should be a part of African American history. It's not how long you live that matters but how you live. My sister was only three years old when she died. This life is a race for some people it's a 100-yard dash and for others it is a marathon. In this life it's not where you finish but how you finish. My sister Josie faced death. I remember the story of the Apostle Paul when he faced a torturing death he was suffering in that prison and ready to meet his maker. I always wondered what pain she felt that day as she died and her face on meeting God that day. I was curious what her reaction was when she saw God as he is and what heaven is like. Me and Josefina have a lot in common. We both came from a hell hole.

Paul states in Romans 6:9 KJV:

Knowing that Christ being raised from the dead dieth no more; death hath no more dominion over him

Book Summary

"The Josefina Catherine Cunningham Memorial," is a heart-wrenching account of the life and tragic death of three-year-old Josefina Catherine Cunningham. Born to an African American family in Rensselaer, New York, Josefina's life was abruptly ended on July 7, 2023, by the hands of a thirty-three-year-old white man, Robert J. Fisher.

The narrative unfolds with the horrifying discovery of Josefina's lifeless body, covered in bleach with blue spots all over her. The family learns of this devastating news through a phone call from Josefina's aunt to her brother. As the investigation progresses, it becomes evident that Josefina was brutally raped and murdered, with the crime scene revealing a violent struggle.

The book emphasizes the importance of Josefina's story being heard, especially in the context of black history, as she was an African American victim of homicidal violence. The last portrait taken of Josefina before her death serves as a poignant reminder of her untimely demise.

Robert Fisher, the accused, has entered a not-guilty plea in the Rensselaer County City Court. While a trial date is yet to be set, the case has garnered significant attention in New York State, with Josefina's family determined to bring her tragic story to international light.

Jyquan Stewart, a family member, is leading a campaign to reinstate the death penalty for child murderers and rapists in New York State. As the trial of Robert J. Fisher unfolds, the horrifying details of Josefina's murder have sent shockwaves through the community, grabbing the nation's attention and igniting a demand for severe consequences for such heinous crimes.

This book serves as a testament to Josefina's memory and a call to action against such atrocities, encapsulating the family's relentless pursuit of justice for Josefina.

{ 1 }

The Birth of Josefina

On a warm summer day, July 25, 2019, in the bustling city of Albany, New York, a new life was welcomed into the world at St. Peter's Memorial Hospital. This life was none other than my sister, Josefina Catherine Cunningham. Born to Lakeisha Stewart and Joseph Cunningham, she was the newest addition to our lineage, a lineage that traced back to our late grandparents, Willie Stewart and Catherine Stewart. The anticipation of Josefina's arrival was a memory etched in my mind. I recall the sensation of her tiny kicks against my mother's belly, a tangible sign of the little life growing within. The news of having a little sister filled me with an excitement that was hard to contain. It was almost unbelievable that our family was about to welcome another member.

The weeks leading up to her birth were filled with preparations and a sense of heightened expectation. I remember my mother meticulously arranging Josefina's nursery, painting the walls a soft pastel pink and filling the room with plush toys and a crib adorned with delicate lace. My father would often be seen assembling furniture or carefully reading baby care books, ensuring he was well-prepared for our new arrival. The house was abuzz with discussions about baby names, the best pediatricians in town, and plans for a grand welcome home party. Each day brought us closer to meeting the little one, and our hearts swelled with love and anticipation.

However, the joyous anticipation was interspersed with moments of anxiety. The labor pains my mother endured were intense, so much so that she had to be rushed to the hospital. What followed were three long days of waiting, days filled with a mix of anxiety and anticipation. Each minute felt like an hour as we camped out in the hospital's waiting room. My aunt, two cousins, and my mother's husband were there, offering support and comfort. We shared stories, played cards, and tried to keep each other's spirits up, but the underlying tension was palpable. Every time a nurse walked by, we held our breath, hoping for news.

On the third day, as I sat in the waiting room, a text message broke the silence: "She is here." Relief washed over us, and we rushed to meet the newest member of our family. The first sight of Josefina was both joyous and concerning. Her tiny body was shaky due to low blood sugar, necessitating her immediate transfer to the Intensive Care Unit (ICU). I remember peering through the glass window of the ICU, my heart aching at the sight of her hooked up to various monitors and tubes. Despite the circumstances, I was overjoyed to finally meet my little sister.

Josefina spent nearly three weeks in the ICU, a period that felt like an eternity. We were constantly in and out of the hospital, balancing our daily lives with visits to see her. The nurses and doctors became familiar faces, and the sterile hospital environment started to feel like a second home. During this time, we discovered another health concern - a heart murmur. This discovery meant that Josefina would need the care of a cardiologist. My parents were understandably worried, but they remained strong and hopeful. They spent hours researching, consulting with specialists, and ensuring that Josefina received the best care possible

Thus began our journey with Josefina, a journey filled with love, concern, and the unwavering hope for her bright future. Despite the challenges, each day brought a small victory. The first time she opened her eyes, her first smile, and eventually, her first trip home. Our family rallied together, offering support and care. Grandparents, aunts, uncles, and cousins all pitched in, creating a web of love and security around Josefina.

The experience brought our family closer together. We celebrated each milestone, no matter how small, and learned to cherish the moments of joy amidst the struggles. My parents' strength and resilience were a source of inspiration for me. Watching them navigate the challenges with unwavering determination taught me the true meaning of family and unconditional love.

Today, as I look at Josefina, a healthy and spirited little girl, I am filled with gratitude. Her journey, though marked with challenges, has been a testament to the power of love and perseverance. Josefina's arrival has forever changed our lives, bringing us closer and reminding us of the preciousness of each moment. She is a constant source of joy and a symbol of the enduring bond that holds our family together.

{ **2** }

Arrival of an Angel

The day Josefina came home from St. Peter's Memorial Hospital in Albany, New York, is etched in my memory. My Aunt Dina had the honor of bringing my mother home from the hospital. As my mother walked through the door, she was greeted by the sight of her house in disarray, which understandably upset her. Amidst this chaos, Josefina was a picture of serenity, sound asleep in her new car seat. The excitement of seeing my little sister for the first time was overwhelming. Despite the initial shock, my mother, Aunt Dina, and I rallied together to restore order to the house. As we cleaned, Josefina continued to sleep peacefully, oblivious to the flurry of activity around her. Josefina's arrival felt like a divine intervention, a beacon of light descending from heaven. She was an angel in every sense of the word. There are instances in the Bible where angels have appeared in human form, and having seen and encountered angels myself, I believe that Josefina's presence in this world had a divine purpose. I believe her purpose was to impact history and narrate a tale of how the church is losing its way, affecting our younger generation. The youth, being the future of our society, are of utmost importance. We seem to be drifting away from the apostolic roots left to us by our ancestors. I can't help but think that this is a consequence of my family's deviation from Christ. This belief strengthens my resolve to ensure that Josefina's story is heard and serves as a wake-up call for all.

Josefina's First Journey: The Beginning of Mobility

My sister Josefina was ten months old, and her growth since birth had been remarkable. At this tender age, she had started crawling and could even say "yes" and "no." Each new milestone she reached was a source of immense joy and pride for our family. The days seemed to pass quickly as we marveled at her development, watching in awe as she explored her surroundings with curiosity and determination. Josefina was still on baby formula, and her pacifier was her constant companion. She would clutch it tightly, her small fingers wrapped around it as if it were the most precious thing in the world. The sight of her with that pacifier, her wide eyes filled with wonder, never failed to melt our hearts. Her adorableness was undeniable, and she had an uncanny ability to bring smiles to the faces of everyone around her.

Whenever our family visited, they were inevitably drawn to Josie, as we affectionately called her. Her cuteness and innocence were captivating, and she had a magnetic presence that attracted people like a magnet. Our home was often filled with laughter and joy as relatives took turns holding her, playing with her, and marveling at her every little action. Josie's infectious laughter and bright eyes brought a sense of warmth and happiness that enveloped everyone in the room.

One of my fondest memories during this time was seeing Josefina in the arms of our cousin Jusiah. Jusiah, a teenager with a typically aloof demeanor, transformed into a gentle giant whenever he held Josefina. The contrast between his towering frame and her tiny body was endearing, and the way he cradled her with such care and tenderness was a sight to behold. Josie seemed to sense his protective nature and would often look up at him with a trusting gaze, her eyes sparkling with affection.

During family gatherings, Josefina became the center of attention. Everyone would gather around her, eager to witness her latest antics. Whether it was her clumsy attempts at crawling or her determined babbling as she tried to communicate, she had a way of making every moment special. Her ability to say "yes" and "no" added a new dimension to our interactions with her. It was both amusing and heartwarming to see her nod or shake her head in response to our questions, her expressions full of earnestness.

Our home was a hive of activity, filled with the sounds of Josie's playful giggles and the chatter of family members. The living room often turned into a makeshift play area, with toys scattered across the floor and adults sitting in a circle, watching Josie explore. She would crawl from one person to another, her face lighting up with excitement each time she discovered something new. Every stumble, every attempt to pull herself up, was met with cheers and encouragement from all of us.

Amidst all the activity, my mother kept a close eye on Josefina, ensuring she was safe and well-cared for. She had developed a keen sense of Josie's needs and could anticipate when she was hungry, tired, or simply in need of a cuddle. The bond between my mother and Josefina was profound, built on a foundation of love and trust. Watching them together was a reminder of the unbreakable connection that forms between a mother and her child.

As the months went by, Josefina's personality began to shine through more vividly. She had a playful spirit and a mischievous streak that kept us all on our toes. Her laughter was infectious, and she had a knack for turning even the simplest moments into sources of joy. Whether it was splashing in her baby bath, playing peek-a-boo, or simply clapping her hands in delight, she brought a sense of wonder to our everyday lives.

Even as she grew, Josie remained inseparable from her pacifier. It was her comfort object, a source of solace in an ever-expanding world. She would often fall asleep with it in her mouth, her breathing slow and steady as she drifted off into peaceful slumber. Those moments of quiet, when the house was still and Josie was asleep, were precious. They allowed us to reflect on how much she had grown and how deeply she had impacted our lives.

Josefina's first ten months were a whirlwind of growth and discovery. She transformed from a fragile newborn into a lively, curious baby. Watching her develop was a privilege, each new skill she acquired a testament to her resilience and spirit. Josie's presence in our family had brought us closer, creating a tapestry of memories woven with love, laughter, and the joy of watching a child grow. As we looked ahead, we knew that each new day with Josefina would continue to be filled with wonder and delight.

Josefina's First Words

At two years old, my sister Josefina began calling me 'brother.' Hearing her sweet voice utter that word for the first time was a moment I'll never forget. It felt like a milestone in our relationship, a signal that she was beginning to understand the familial bonds that connected us. Josefina's intelligence was evident early on; she was capable of normal conversation, astonishing us with her ability to grasp language and express her thoughts and feelings.

Josie, as we affectionately called her, was a lively and curious child. Her capacity for understanding and engaging with the world around her was truly remarkable. Conversations with her were often filled with wonder as she asked questions about everything she saw, wanting to know the names of objects and their purposes. She was like a little sponge, soaking up information with an eagerness that was both endearing and impressive.

One of Josefina's favorite activities was singing, and her song of choice was the ever-popular 'Baby Shark.' She would sing it at the top of her lungs, her tiny voice filling the house with infectious energy. No matter how many times we heard it, her rendition never failed to bring smiles to our faces. Her enthusiasm was contagious, and it wasn't long before the entire family would join in, creating a fun and lively atmosphere. 'Baby Shark' became a sort of family anthem, a song that symbolized the joy and togetherness we shared.

In addition to her love for singing, Josefina was always on the move. She loved running around, her little legs carrying her from one room to another with boundless energy. Her laughter echoed through the house as she played, her joy evident in every giggle and squeal of delight. Watching her run around was like witnessing pure happiness in motion. She had a way of turning even the most mundane activities into adventures, and her zest for life was a constant source of inspiration.

Playing with her toys was another favorite pastime. Josefina had a vast collection of toys, each one cherished and played with in a way that brought them to life. Whether it was building elaborate structures with her blocks, hosting tea parties with her stuffed animals, or creating intricate stories with her dolls, she immersed herself fully in her play. Her imagination knew no bounds, and she often invited us to join her in her make-believe worlds. These moments of play were special, as they allowed us to see the world through her eyes, a world filled with endless possibilities and unbridled creativity.

Her toys were not just objects to her; they were companions in her adventures. Each toy had a personality and a story, and she would narrate these stories with great enthusiasm. It was fascinating to watch her mind at work, constructing narratives that were both complex and whimsical. Her creativity and storytelling ability were truly remarkable, and it was clear that she saw the world as a place brimming with potential and magic.

Josefina's energy and intelligence were balanced by her affectionate nature. She had a way of making everyone around her feel special and loved. Her hugs were warm and sincere, and she would often come up to me, her big brown eyes looking up with a smile, and say, 'I love you, brother.' Those words, so simple yet so profound, had a way of melting my heart. Her love was pure and unconditional, and it was a constant reminder of the importance of family and the bonds we share.

As she continued to grow, her personality blossomed even more. She became more confident and assertive, her voice reflecting her growing sense of self. She developed preferences and opinions, and she wasn't shy about expressing them. Whether it was choosing her favorite outfit or deciding what game to play, Josefina approached every decision with a combination of thoughtfulness and determination. Her assertiveness was admirable, and it was clear that she was becoming her own person, with her own unique identity.

Looking back at those early years, it's clear that Josefina brought an immense amount of joy and light into our lives. Her intelligence, energy, and affectionate nature made every day special. She taught us to appreciate the little things, to find joy in the simplest moments, and to always approach life with a sense of wonder and curiosity. Her laughter, her songs, and her stories created a tapestry of memories that we will cherish forever. Josefina's presence was a gift, a reminder of the beauty and innocence of childhood, and the incredible bond that siblings share.

Josefina at age three and her death.

In the bustling city of Albany, New York, nestled within the warm walls of Victory Day Care, little Josefina's laughter was a familiar melody. At the tender age of three, her world was a tapestry of simple joys and loving bonds. It was here, amidst the innocent chaos of childhood, that she uttered words that would forever echo in my heart "That's my brother." A declaration so pure that it imprinted an indelible memory.

Josefina's voice, a sweet chime over the phone, would greet me with a cheerful "Hi brother," followed by the curious, "What are you doing?" Each visit to their mother's home was a celebration of sibling love, marked by Josefina's eager embrace and a parting kiss that whispered "bye" brother. These moments, though fleeting, held the weight of eternity. Tragedy struck in the neighboring town of Rensselaer, New York where the day before Josefina's untimely departure from this world; she radiated the essence of health and vitality. However, a shadow loomed in the form of Robert J. Fisher, our mother's new companion, whose inebriated state foreshadowed the impending sorrow. With our mother, Lakeisha Stewart, away at Walmart, Josefina's safety was left in the hands of a man ill-equipped to care for her.

The night before Josefina's death is a haunting memory etched into my mind. I had gone to our mother's house to retrieve my keys, unaware that it would be the last time I would see my sister alive. Josefina had been left alone in the house with Fisher while our mother made a quick trip to Walmart. When she returned, she found Josefina sound asleep, seemingly safe and secure. Little did she know, the night would take a horrifying turn.

In the middle of the night, our mother discovered Fisher deleting items from his phone while lying naked on the couch. Startled and confused, she covered him with a towel, oblivious to the unspeakable horrors that had already transpired. The following morning brought an unimaginable nightmare. Our mother found Josefina's lifeless body, covered in bleach and with blue spots marking her delicate skin. The sight was beyond comprehension, a scene from the darkest of nightmares.

In a state of panic, our mother called 911, her voice trembling with a mix of terror and heart-break. As she wept uncontrollably, Fisher remained eerily composed, showing no signs of distress or grief. His cold demeanor was chilling, a stark contrast to the devastation that had engulfed our family. The Rensselaer Police Department quickly responded, securing the area and ordering everyone to leave the house. Despite the ongoing investigation, Robert Fisher attempted to re-enter the home, leading to his immediate arrest and subsequent questioning by the police.

The devastating news reached me in the most abrupt and heart-wrenching manner. I was on my way to work when our aunt called, her voice heavy with sorrow. "Did you know that Josie died?" she asked. The world seemed to stop, and a wave of disbelief washed over me. My mind struggled to process the information, and I felt an overwhelming sense of loss and helplessness.

When I arrived at my mother's house, I was met with a grim scene: a heavy police presence, crime scene tape cordoning off the area, and the somber faces of neighbors and relatives. The air was thick with grief and shock. At Albany Medical Center, Detective Michael Deso of the Rensselaer Police Department was present, offering his support and condolences. His presence was a small comfort in the midst of chaos, a reminder that we were not alone in our grief.

As the investigation unfolded, the horrific details of Josefina's last moments began to emerge. It became painfully clear that she had been brutally raped and murdered. The crime scene revealed blood on the bed, indicating a violent struggle. The realization that such evil had invaded our home was shattering. Josefina's innocence and light had been extinguished in the most cruel and inhumane manner.

Our family was plunged into an abyss of sorrow and anger. We were left grappling with the enormity of our loss and the sheer brutality of the crime. Josefina had been a beacon of joy and love in our lives, and her death left a void that could never be filled. As we mourned her loss, we also sought justice for her. We demanded that the world hear her story, that her death not be in vain. We wanted to stand against such heinous acts, to ensure that no other family would endure the same pain.

The community rallied around us, offering support and solidarity. Vigils were held in Josefina's memory, and her story spread beyond our town, resonating with people who were horrified by the senseless violence. The media coverage helped bring attention to the issue, highlighting the urgent need for justice and reform.

Through our grief, we found a collective strength. We became advocates for change, determined to honor Josefina's memory by fighting for a safer world. We engaged with lawmakers, supported organizations working to prevent violence, and shared Josefina's story widely. Her life, though tragically short, became a catalyst for awareness and action.

The journey towards justice was long and arduous, marked by court hearings and emotional testimonies. Fisher's trial was a grueling process, but our resolve never wavered. We stood united, driven by the love we had for Josefina and the desire to see her killer held accountable. In the end, Josefina's legacy was one of resilience and love. Her story became a powerful reminder of the need for vigilance, compassion, and action. We vowed to keep her memory alive, to ensure that her light would continue to shine through our efforts to create a better world.

1552 BROADWAY IN RENSSELAER, NEW YOEK WHERE JOSIE DIED.

Capt. Robert Appleton of New York State Troopers

Funeral of Josefina Catherine Cunningham

I recall entering the W.J. Lyons Funeral Home in Rensselaer, New York. I was the first to arrive at my sister's funeral. She had been cremated, and her urns were before me. As I walked into the funeral home, I sensed God's presence. It was clear to me that my sister had completed her journey. My mother was weeping intensely; it was the most grief-stricken I had ever seen her. Members of the Rensselaer Police and Fire Department were present to pay their respects to Josefina. The funeral service for Josefina was profoundly moving.

Condolences of Josefina Catherine Cunningham

This tree is to honor little Josefina Cunningham - who is now safe in the arms of Jesus. God bless and protect her surviving siblings always.

   - Letty R.

We are deeply sorry for your loss
   ~ the staff at W.J. Lyons Jr. Funeral Home, Inc.

My heartfelt sympathy goes out to the family during this difficult time. Keisha & family, I pray they God will grant you peace in HIS time. Josie rest in peace -gentle soul.

   -Aunt Hattie

Josefina, one of GODS beautiful ANGELS. A Life taken away to soon I'm sending Prayers and Blessings for you sweet Babygirl. May you watch over those who love you? Rest in peace, Josefina

   - Lolita Keyes

At the Rensselaer County City Court

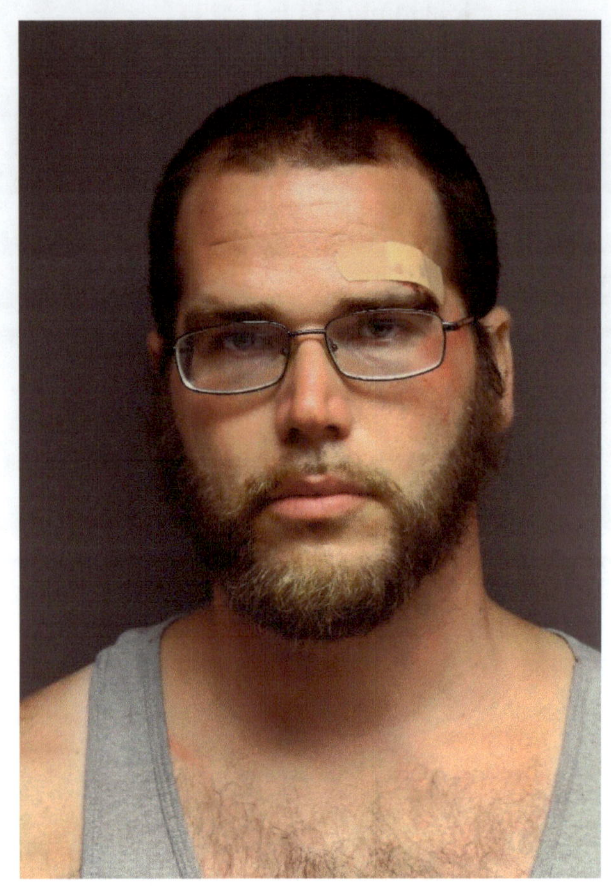